# THE WEATHER REPORT

# TORNADO ALERT!

EDITED BY JOANNE RANDOLPH

SUNDAY MONDAY TUESDAY WEDNESDAY THURSDAY FRIDAY SATURDAY

This edition published in 2018 by:
Enslow Publishing, LLC.
101 W. 23rd Street, Suite 240
New York, NY 10011

Additional materials copyright © 2018 by Enslow Publishing, LLC

**Cataloging-in-Publication Data**

Names: Randolph, Joanne, editor.
Title: Tornado alert! / edited by Joanne Randolph.
Description: New York : Enslow Publishing, 2018 | Series: The weather report | Includes index and bibliographical references. | Audience: Grades 3-5.
Identifiers: ISBN 9780766090279 (library bound) | ISBN 9780766090255 (pbk.) | ISBN 9780766090262 (6 pack)
Subjects: LCSH: Tornadoes--Juvenile literature.
Classification: LCC QC955.2 T67 2018 | DDC 551.55/3—dc23Printed in the United States of America

**To Our Readers:** We have done our best to make sure all website addresses in this book were active and appropriate when we went to press. However, the author and the publisher have no control over and assume no liability for the material available on those websites or on any websites they may link to. Any comments or suggestions can be sent by e-mail to customerservice@enslow.com.

# CONTENTS

# CHAPTER ONE

# ANATOMY OF A TORNADO

You have likely heard of tornadoes, but you may wonder what, exactly, a tornado is. A tornado is a violently whirling column of wind that extends from Earth's surface to the base of a thundercloud. How do you get a rotating column of air? This happens when a wall of warm, moist air meets a wall of cool, dry air. When these air masses collide, the warmer air goes up and the cool air goes under. Updrafts of warm air can reach wind speeds of more than 100 miles (161 kilometers) per hour (mph), sending the warm, moist air miles up into the sky before colliding with the cooler jet stream.

Tornadoes are long columns of air that reach the ground from a thundercloud. The whirling mass of air can destroy anything in its path.

This movement of air masses can create huge rotating storm clouds called **supercells**, resulting in severe weather—high winds, lightning, thunder, heavy rains, and possibly hail (as moisture freezes in the upper **atmosphere**).

## KEEPING AN EYE OUT

**Meteorologists** call the rotation in a supercell a **mesocyclone**. When this circular motion is picked up on radar screens, the National Weather Service (NWS) issues a tornado warning, which means that tornadoes could form and/or that one has been spotted on the ground.

Clouds swirling with rotating funnel clouds hanging down indicate that a tornado could form at any moment. Winds blowing in opposite directions around a strong updraft start a narrow, violent whirl. As **centrifugal** force throws the air away from the center, it leaves a core of very low **air pressure**, which acts as a powerful **vacuum**.

The first sign of a tornado may be a strong whirlwind of dust from the ground's surface. Often, at the same time, a short funnel grows from the storm cloud above it. The funnel becomes more organized, connecting with the rotating column on the ground—and a tornado is born.

If you see a mesocyclone like this one headed your way, take cover. A tornado may soon be on its way.

Supercell thunderstorms are a tornado warning sign. This supercell in Colorado produced two tornadoes.

# HOW ARE THEY MEASURED?

How are tornadoes measured? Meteorologists use the Enhanced Fujita Scale. Since it is currently impossible to measure wind speed in the **vortex** of a tornado, the EF-Scale is based on damage done by the twister.

| SCALE | WIND ESTIMATE MPH (KMH) | TYPICAL DAMAGE |
|-------|-------------------------|----------------|
| EF0 | 65-85 (105-137) | Minor or none |
| EF1 | 86-110 (138-177) | Moderate |
| EF2 | 111-135 (178-217) | Significant |
| EF3 | 136-165 (218-266) | Severe |
| EF4 | 166-200 (267-322) | Devastating |
| EF5 | >200 (>323) | Incredible |

# CHAPTER TWO

# GAZING INTO A CRYSTAL BALL

Meteorologists rely on many tools to predict, track, and warn us about storms. **Doppler radar** can tell meteorologists how fast winds are moving and in what direction. Satellites give a big-picture view of the atmosphere from above, and most airports and airplanes take regular measurements of wind speed, direction, and pressure. All of these data feed into computer models of the atmosphere that run **simulations** to help us understand how the weather will change over the next few days. "They're like our crystal ball," says Greg Carbin of the NWS Storm Prediction Center in Oklahoma.

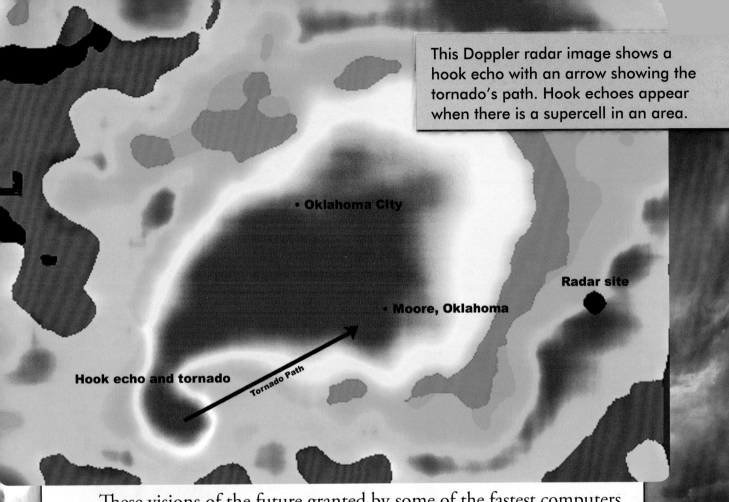

This Doppler radar image shows a hook echo with an arrow showing the tornado's path. Hook echoes appear when there is a supercell in an area.

• Oklahoma City

Radar site

• Moore, Oklahoma

Hook echo and tornado

Tornado Path

These visions of the future granted by some of the fastest computers in the world still aren't perfect. The simulations can't possibly handle data from every single point in the atmosphere, so they average the numbers across large areas. Tornadoes are especially tricky to predict simply because of their small size. "Tornadoes are terrible and tiny," says Carbin, "and hurricanes are horrible and huge." That's why we get a hurricane warning

This satellite image from space shows 2016's gigantic Hurricane Matthew barreling toward Florida.

several days in advance, but a tornado warning often comes only twenty to thirty minutes before the storm.

In the next few years, computer modeling could reach small scales of 5 to 10 miles (8 to 16 kilometers), and eventually, it could become possible to model and predict individual thunderstorms. "You really need the best and brightest programmers and the fastest computers to do that type of work," says Carbin.

## TRACKING THE BEAST

With Doppler radar linked to a bank of computers, the NWS has the capability to detect supercell thunderstorms and track their movement. Doppler radar runs in two modes. In one, the storm reflects energy back to the radar showing how intense the storm is. The second is much like police radar—a beam is sent out and bounces back with a different frequency. The change in frequency allows the radar to determine movement toward or away from the radar, thus detecting rotation in the supercell.

The NWS also utilizes data from weather satellites. But even with all these up-to-date methods and equipment, human beings are still a vital part of severe weather prediction and early warning. People are needed to interpret the information, and storm spotters and chasers are needed at the scene.

Weather satellites help meteorologists provide advanced warning for extreme weather events, such as tornadoes.

## SPOTTING AND CHASING THE BEAST

Spotters and chasers? These aren't just thrill-seekers out to see how close they can get to a tornado without being swallowed up. These people have been trained to assess the elements of supercells and identify tornadoes as they form. Spotters follow storms to watch for this development. They have also been taught how to "chase" a storm, while leaving themselves an escape route should the monster winds turn toward them.

This exciting and dangerous aspect of weather watching plays an important part in the safety of many communities. The spotters and chasers send their information to the NWS, which turns it into reports and broadcasts these updates on the emergency broadcasting network and National Oceanographic and Atmospheric Administration (NOAA) weather radio stations.

Roger Hill has chased and photographed countless tornadoes in the midwestern region of the country. He has been a storm chaser for more than thirty years.

# CHAPTER THREE

# TERRIBLE TWISTER: AN INSIDER'S LOOK AT A TORNADO

Winds shrieking and swirling at more than 210 miles (338 km) per hour, a giant tornado bore down on the city of Joplin, Missouri, around 5:40 p.m. on May 22, 2011. Directly in its path, twelve-year-old Caleb, his parents, and his two little sisters sat at the local Stained Glass Theater watching a play. "The air got this funny feel and my mom started telling me that we'd better get down to the basement," Caleb said. He was one of only five people who made it inside the storage room, the closest thing to a storm room in the theater. Almost everyone else huddled in the basement, the stairwell, or on the auditorium floor by the stage.

This motel with the classic Thunderbird cars is in Joplin, Missouri. The city was hit by a tornado in 2011.

15

# Inside the Cyclone

"It was terrible. I plugged my ears and started yelling," said Caleb.

Moving at 20 to 25 miles (32 to 40 km) per hour, slow for a tornado, it took the storm about a minute to tear through the theater, ripping off the roof and walls, snapping the plank of wood securing the back door, and smashing cars against the foundation.

"It felt like an eternity," Caleb said. "I was pretty sure someone in my family was going to die."

Miraculously, his family all survived with minor bumps, cuts, and bruises. A friend of Caleb's who was also at the theater had to be air-lifted to a hospital in Kansas City because of injuries. The hospital next door to the theater, St. John's, was too badly damaged to treat anyone. The friend recovered, and Caleb's house, just a fifteen-minute drive from the theater, was untouched.

What makes a storm like the Joplin tornado possible? How in the world does an atmosphere that most of the time provides us with sunshine, a few rain showers, and pleasant breezes, wrap a car around a telephone pole?

# Recipe for Disaster

To make a tornado, first you need an unstable atmosphere, with a lot of **convective available potential energy**, or CAPE. The three key ingredients for CAPE are:

1) **moisture**—extra water suspended in the air, especially near the ground
2) **temperature difference**—warm, moist air below cold, dry air
3) **lift**—a force that makes an air mass rise, such as low pressure

Mix these three together, and the mass of warm, moist air near the ground rises in updrafts that can become very strong. At the same time, cool air from above moves downward. Another thing that increases CAPE is **convective inhibition (CIN)**, which is like a cap on the updrafts. Once the cap breaks, things can get wild. Then, you'll need a fourth ingredient:

4) **wind shear**—winds that get faster and change direction as you go higher in the atmosphere

Shear can tilt the rising updrafts so that the rain and hail fall out of them, and don't slow things down with their weight. All this energy can feed a supercell and the spinning mesocyclone inside. Once you've got a mesocyclone, you'll likely see lightning, thunder, rain, and maybe even hail. As the winds in the mesocyclone high above the ground spin faster and faster, it's likely to form a tornado.

17

The EF-5 level tornado that smashed its way through Joplin, Missouri, left behind this overturned car and debris.

## JOPLIN'S TORNADO—IT'S A 5!

Tornadoes come in many varieties, measured on the Enhanced Fujita Scale (see page 7). The tornado that hit Joplin came in at EF-5, the strongest storm on the scale. What made it so deadly? "Just like any recipe, when you modify the ingredients somewhat, you end up with either a really great dish or a disaster," explains Carbin. It was clear on May 22, 2011, that all the ingredients for wild weather were in place. But the atmosphere is a complex system, and it's very difficult to determine exactly how those four ingredients will interact or how bad a particular storm will actually be until it hits.

## A Year That Broke Records

The Joplin tornado was the deadliest tornado to hit the United States since 1947, but that wasn't the only tornado record set in 2011. A staggering number of tornadoes swept through midwestern and southern states during the last two weeks of April, resulting in a record-breaking 753 total tornadoes that month.

"It was the worst [storm season] I have ever seen," said Howard Bluestein, a storm chaser and professor at the University of Oklahoma.

April and May are normally busy months for severe weather in an area of the United States nicknamed "Tornado Alley." With the Rocky Mountains to the west, the Gulf of Mexico to the south, and the Great Plains in the middle, geography helps create the ingredients for violent weather. As the cold, dry air of the **jet stream** flows west across the United States, it hits the Rocky Mountains, and low pressure forms at their base. This low pressure pulls up warm, moist air from the Gulf of Mexico, which is carried across the open plains, where it slams into the jet stream.

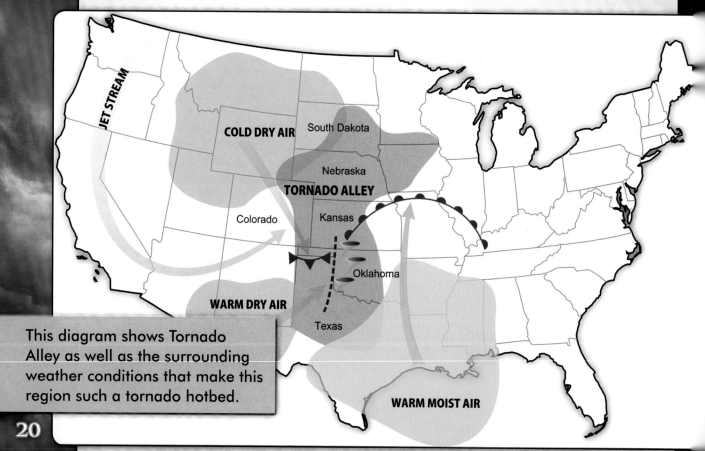

This diagram shows Tornado Alley as well as the surrounding weather conditions that make this region such a tornado hotbed.

Construction workers build a safe room for the home they are rebuilding. The house was destroyed by a tornado in Moore, Oklahoma.

## LIFE WILL NEVER FEEL NORMAL AGAIN

Caleb's family returned home after the storm, but many in Joplin weren't so lucky. Friends who'd lost their house moved in with Caleb's family for three months, and the outpouring of help for victims was incredible. "Our church set up a supply tent where tornado victims could come in any time for free stuff," said Caleb. Still, things will never feel normal again. "Now, whenever there's a storm, I start to panic," he says. Hopefully, he'll never have to endure another tornado, but if one comes, he'll be ready. His family has a safe room in their house, and now they know how serious a tornado warning can be!

# CHAPTER FOUR

# A TWISTER IS COMING!

Tornado safety starts with knowing that a tornado is on its way. And you don't have to live in Tornado Alley to experience a tornado. In 1953, two of the deadliest twisters in United States history occurred in Worcester, Massachusetts, and Flint, Michigan. So wherever you live, stay informed and have a plan.

If a twister is coming and you're in a building:

- **Find the safest place!** If there is no basement, choose a closet, bathroom, or windowless room on the lowest floor, close to the center of the structure.

This tornado in Dodge City, Kansas, was one of about thirty spotted on May 24, 2015, in several different states.

A basement or cellar is a good place to go if there are tornado warnings in your area. Some people have special storm cellars built, specifically to stay safe in frequent tornado zones.

- **Take cover!** If you can, get under something sturdy. Make sure nothing heavy can fall directly on you. Crouch facedown, and cover the back of your neck and head with blankets, pillows, or if nothing else is available, your hands to protect yourself from flying objects—glass, metal, wood, etc.
- **Keep them closed!** Opening doors and windows does not prevent damage and exposes you to more flying debris

Heeding a tornado warning, these teenagers take cover in a bathroom at a local gas station in Wichita, Kansas.

25

A car is not a safe place to be during a tornado. This car's door is open indicating the passengers have left the vehicle to find a safer spot to wait out the storm.

If you're in a car and can't drive away:

- **Get out!** Tornadoes can throw vehicles around like toys. Park off the road so that you don't block the way for emergency vehicles.
- **Get low!** Lie face down in a ditch or low spot. Wind speed is lower at ground level. (If heavy rain is present, watch for flash flooding in your ditch!)
- **Cover up!** Protect your head and neck from flying debris.

There's no way to stop a tornado from wreaking havoc in a community, but being prepared will increase your chances of coming out of it alive.

# GLOSSARY

**air pressure**  The amount of force from Earth's atmosphere on a given point.

**atmosphere**  The blanket of air that surrounds Earth or other planets.

**centrifugal**  Moving outward from the center.

**convective available potential energy (CAPE)**  A measurement of how much energy is waiting to be released in the atmosphere.

**convective inhibition (CIN)**  A measurement of how much energy is preventing air masses from rising upward.

**Doppler radar**  A device meteorologists use to see how fast winds are moving and in what direction.

**jet stream**  A band of westerly flowing air currents that travel around Earth several miles up in the atmosphere.

**mesocyclone** A cyclonic air mass associated with a supercell; its presence is a condition for an tornado warning.

**meteorologist** A scientist who studies the weather.

**simulation** An imitation of a real world process or system.

**supercell** A system producing severe thunderstorms and featuring rotating winds kept up by a long updraft that may result in hail or tornadoes.

**wind shear** Winds that change speed or direction as you go higher in the atmosphere.

**vacuum** A space that has no matter.

**vortex** A spiral mass of air (or water) that sucks everything toward its center.

# FURTHER READING

## Books

Challoner, Jack. *DK Eyewitness Books: Hurricane & Tornado*. New York, NY: DK Children, 2014.

Raum, Elizabeth. *Tornado!* Mankato, MN: Amicus High Interest, 2016.

Simon, Seymour. *Tornadoes*. New York, NY: HarperCollins, 2017.

Tarshis, Lauren. *Tornado Terror*. New York, NY: Scholastic Press, 2017.

## WEBSITES

**The National Severe Storms Laboratory**

*www.nssl.noaa.gov/education/svrwx101/tornadoes*

Learn more information about tornadoes.

**Ready, Tornadoes**

*www.ready.gov/tornadoes*

This government website explains what you should do before and during a tornado.

**Weather Wiz Kids**

*www.weatherwizkids.com/weather-tornado.htm*

Read about how tornadoes form, where they are most likely to occur, and other data about these storms.

# INDEX